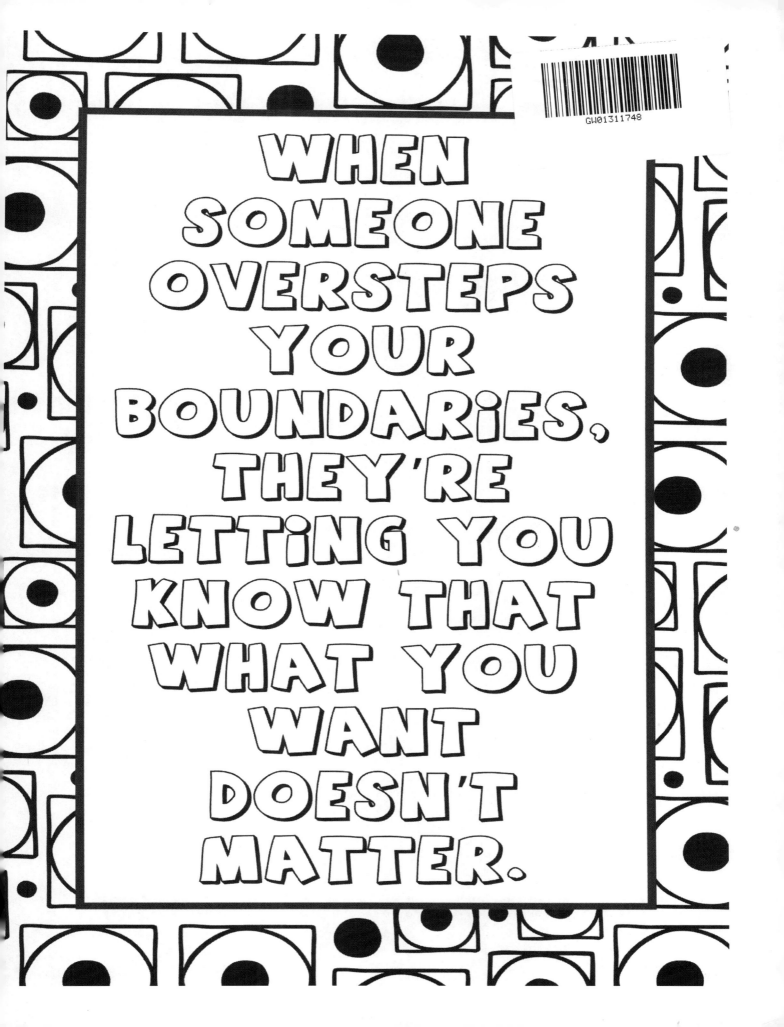

A NARCISSISTS LOVES OTHERS BASED SOLELY ON WHAT YOU CAN DO FOR THEM.

PLAYING THE VICTIM ROLE, A MANIPULATOR PORTRAYS HIM OR HERSELF AS A VICTIM

MAKE SURE EVERYBODY IN YOUR "BOAT" IS ROWING AND NOT DRILLING HOLES WHEN YOU'RE NOT LOOKING.

WHEN A TOXIC PERSON CAN NO LONGER CONTROL YOU, THEY WILL TRY TO CONTROL HOW OTHERS SEE YOU.

ARGUING WITH A NARCISSIST IS LIKE GETTING ARRESTED. EVERYTHING YOU DO OR SAY WILL BE HELD AGAINST YOU.

"NARCISSISTIC LOVE IS RIDING ON THE ROLLERCOASTER OF DISASTER FILLED WITH A HEART FULL OF TEARS."

— SHEREE GRIFFIN

YOU ARE NOT CRAZY

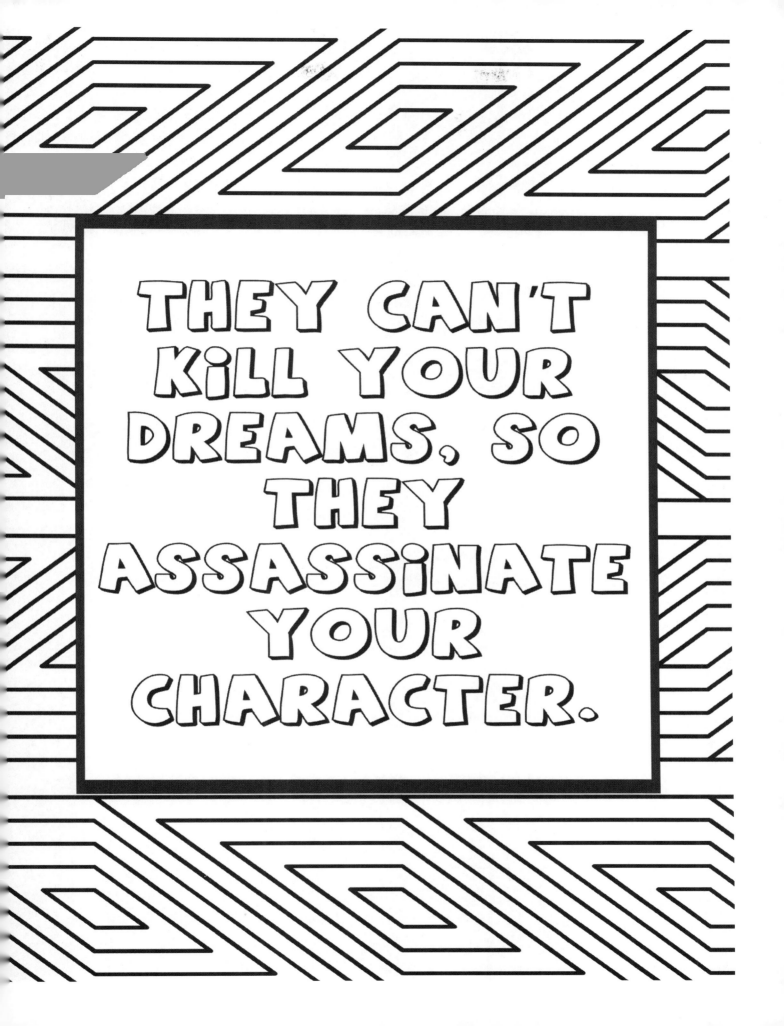

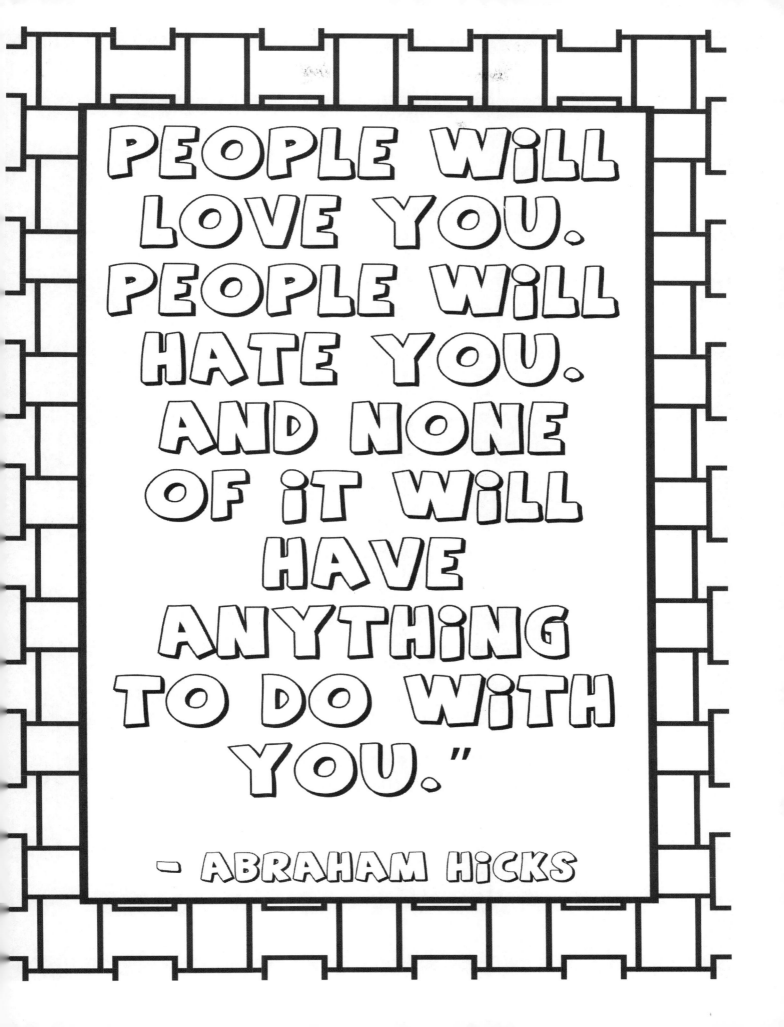

THOSE WHO SAY IT COSTS NOTHING TO BE KIND HAVEN'T MET A NARCISSIST.

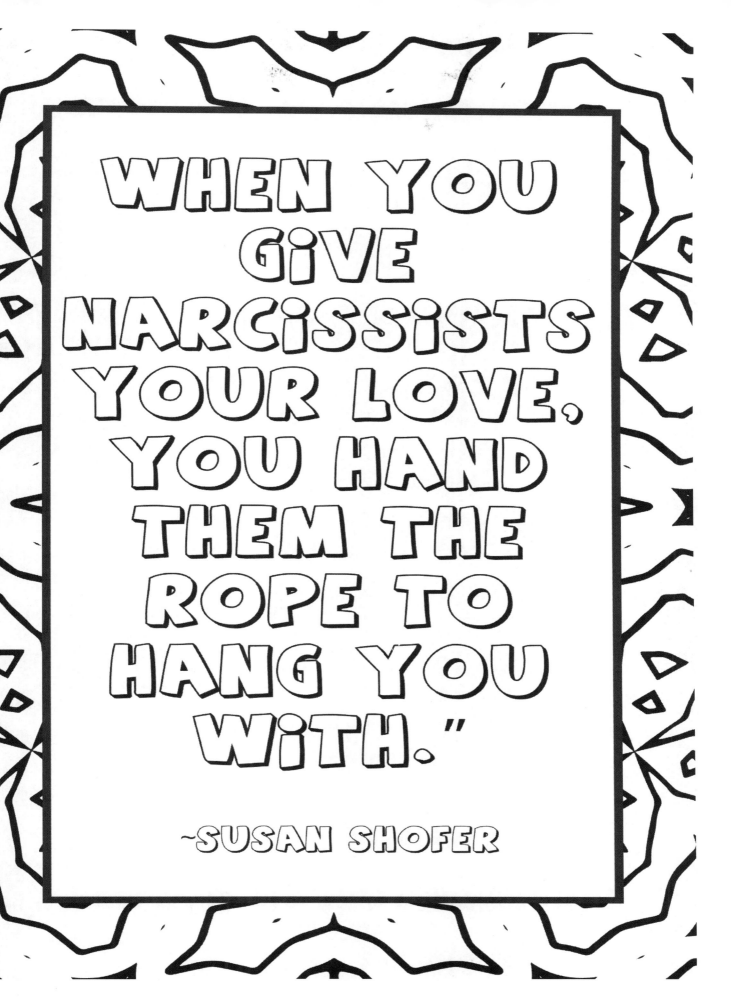

"WHEN YOU GIVE NARCISSISTS YOUR LOVE, YOU HAND THEM THE ROPE TO HANG YOU WITH."

~SUSAN SHOFER

GAS-LIGHTING

THEY WILL TELL YOU IT'S ALL IN YOUR HEAD AND YOU ARE THE PROBLEM.

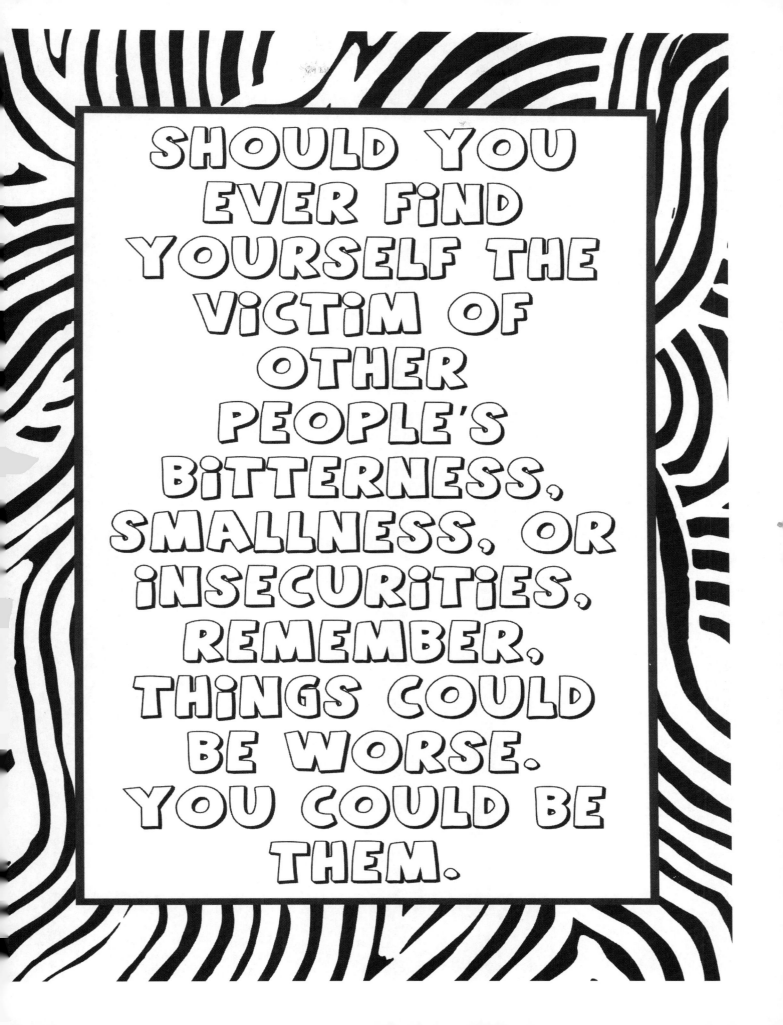

HOW BEAUTIFUL IT IS TO STAY SILENT WHEN SOMEONE EXPECTS YOU TO BE ENRAGED.

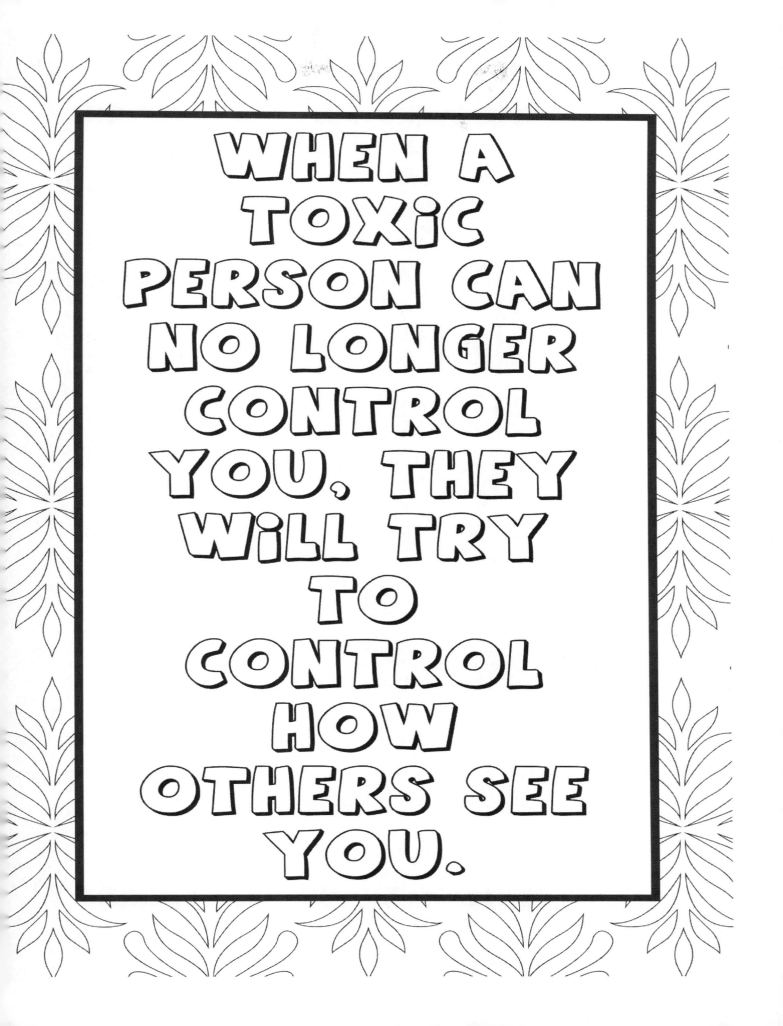

EVER NOTICED HOW A NARCISSIST'S CONVERSATIONS ALWAYS CIRCLE BACK TO THEM

THEY SAY THE MOST BEAUTIFUL THING A NARCISSIST CAN SEE IS THEIR OWN REFLECTION

> NOBODY CAN BE KINDER THAN THE NARCISSIST WHILE YOU REACT TO LIFE ON HIS TERMS.
>
> — ELIZABETH BOWEN

> Sometimes it's not the people who change; it's the mask that falls off.
>
> — Haruki Murakami

NARCISSISTS LIKE BEING FEARED.

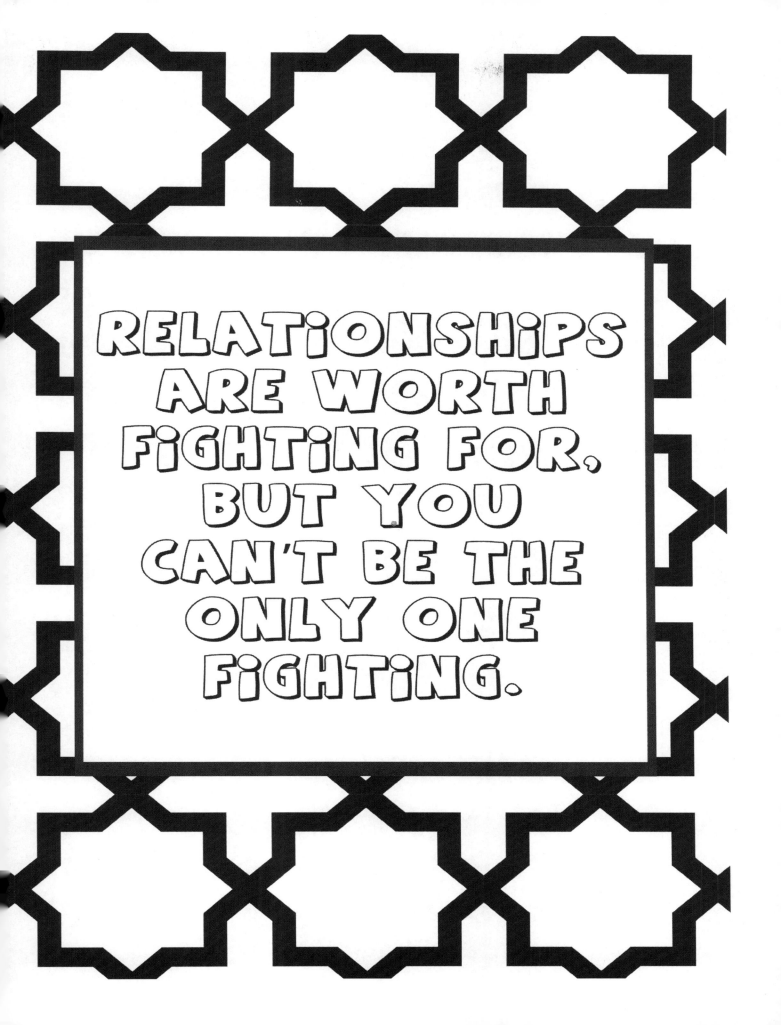

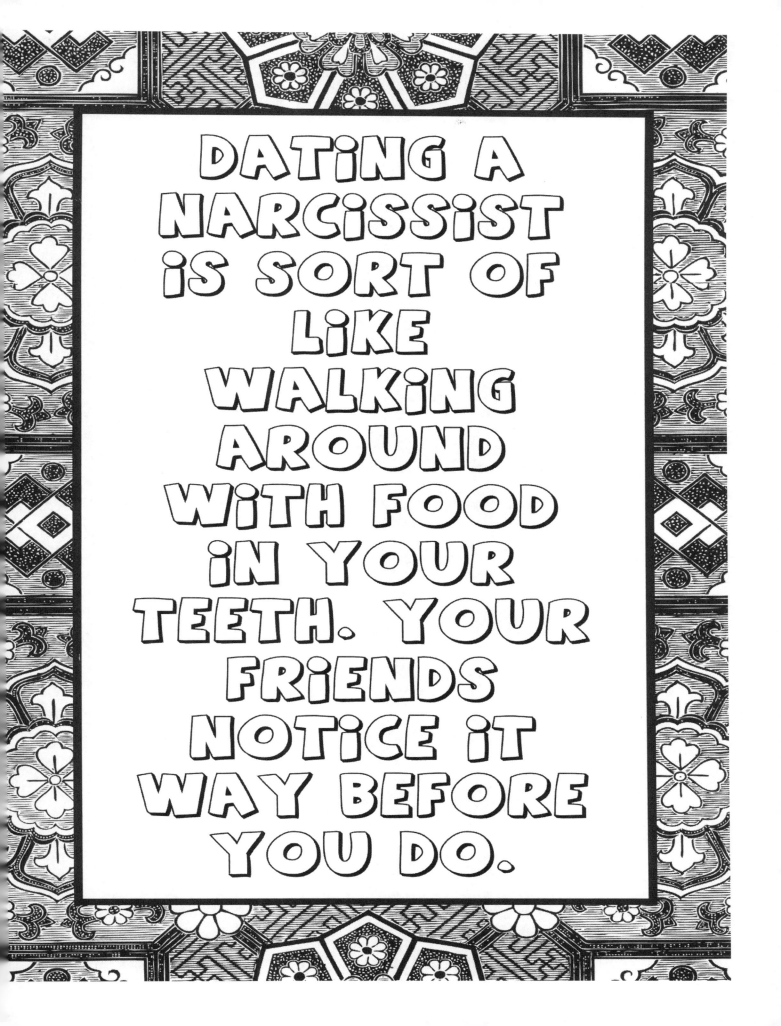

PAY ATTENTION TO THE PEOPLE WHO DON'T CLAP WHEN YOU WIN.

WHEN PEOPLE SAY, "YOU'VE CHANGED," THERE'S A CHANCE THAT YOU JUST STOPPED ACTING THE WAY THEY WANTED YOU TO.

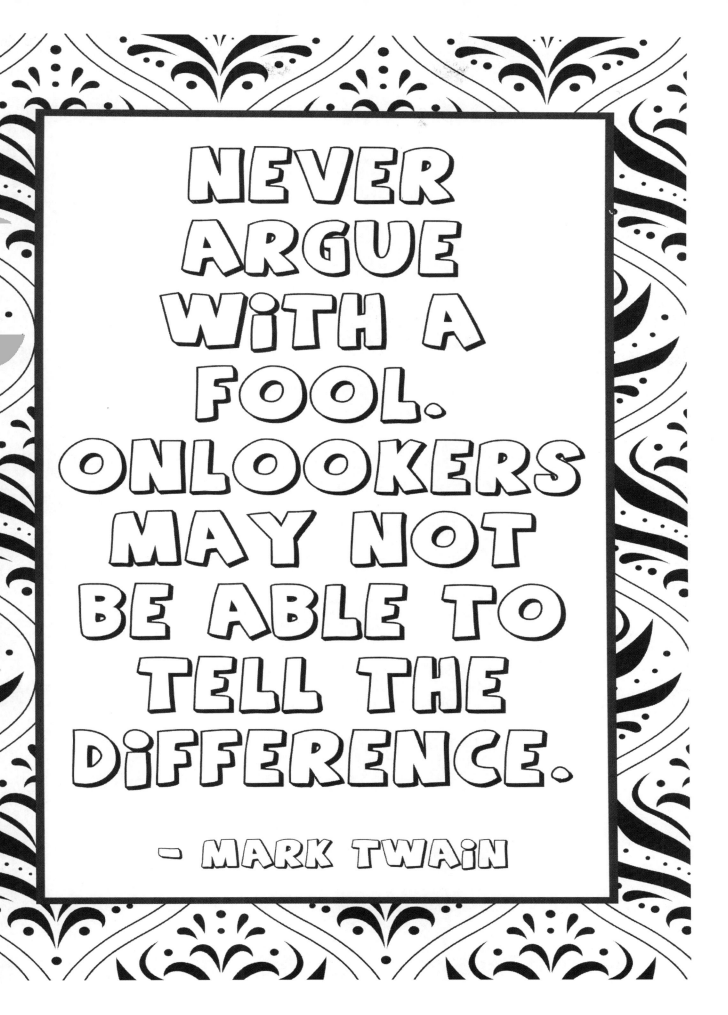

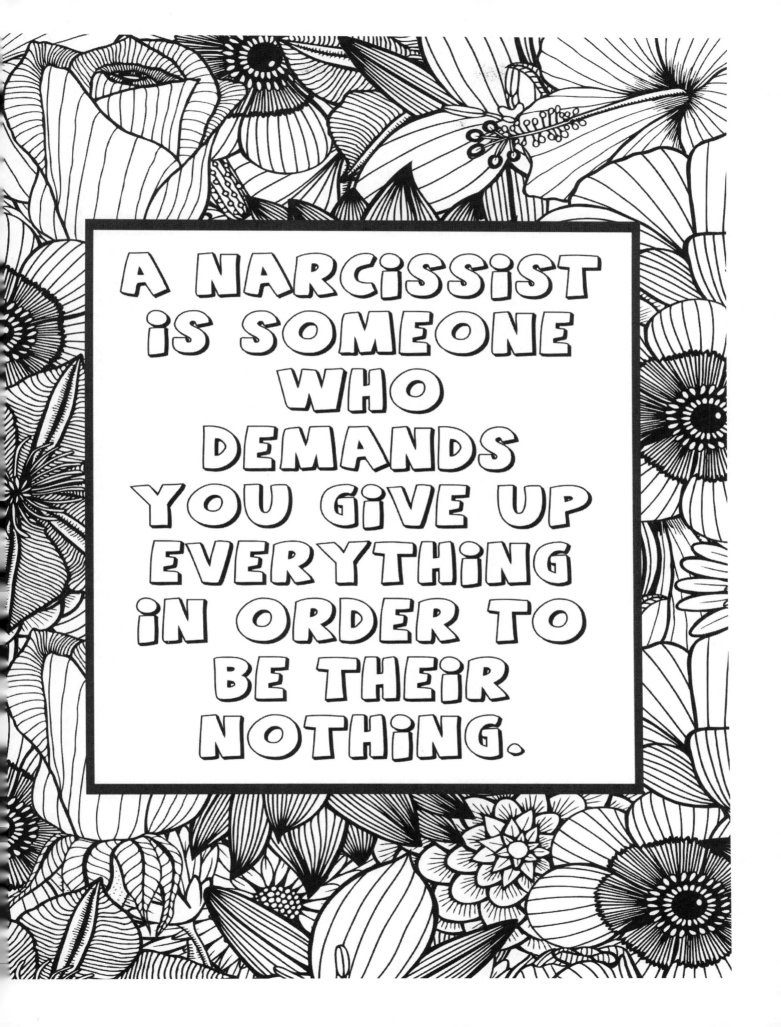

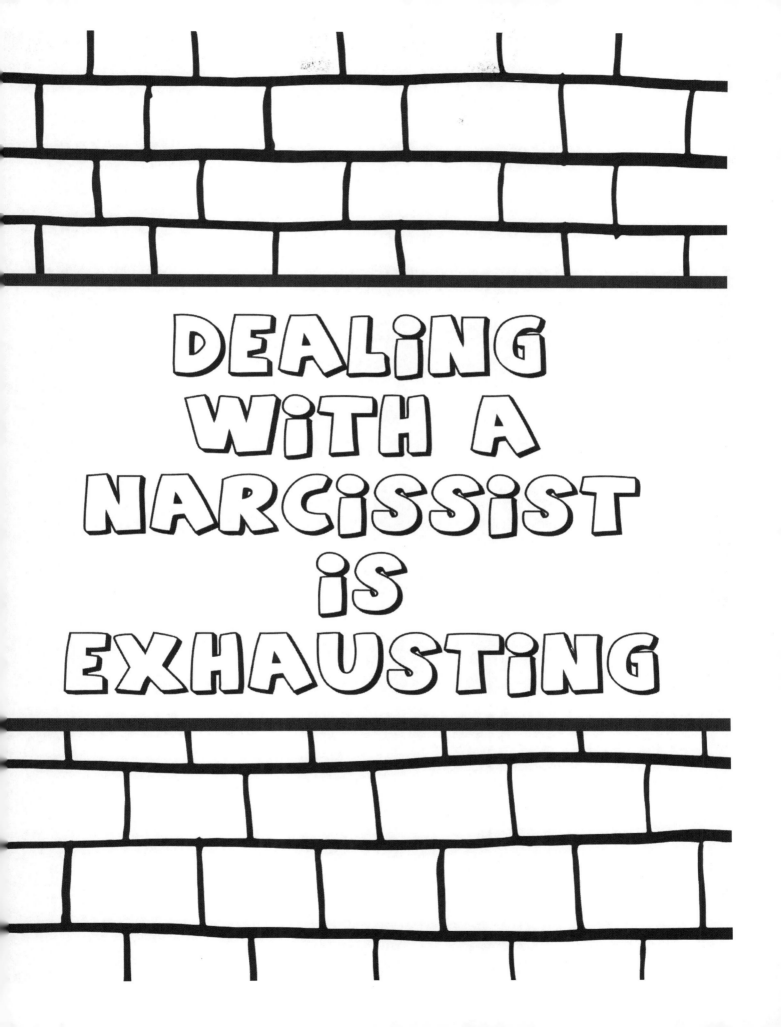

i knew without a shadow of a doubt that no matter what i said or did, nothing was going to change.

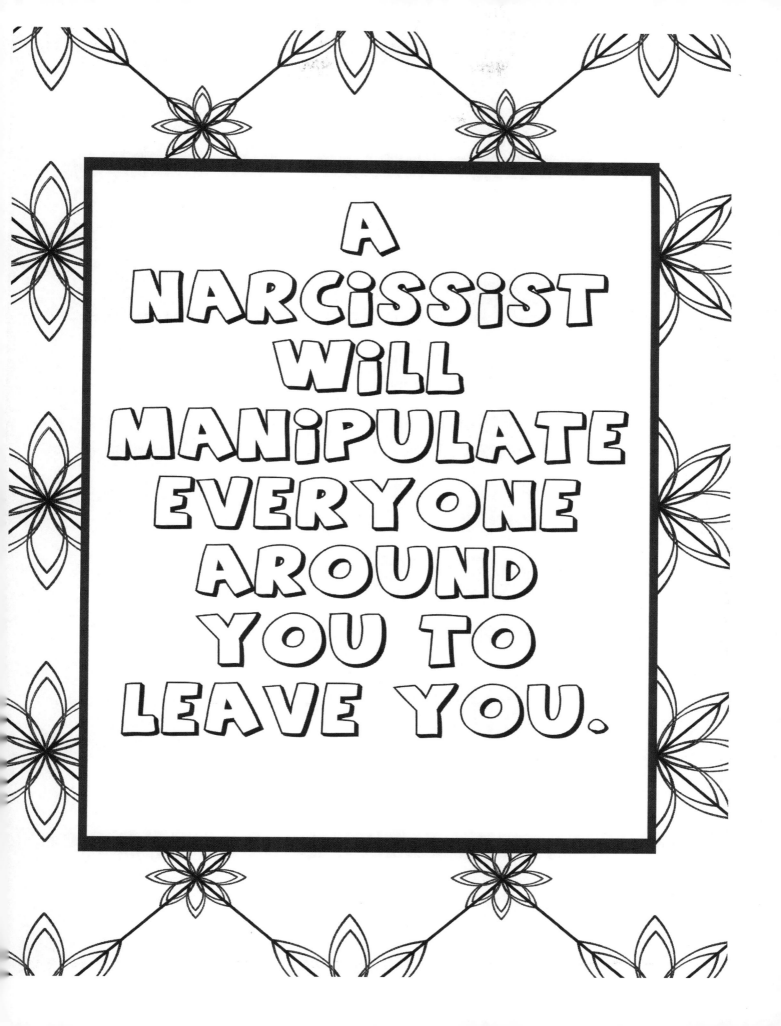

THE ONLY WAY TO WIN WITH A TOXIC PERSON IS NOT TO PLAY.

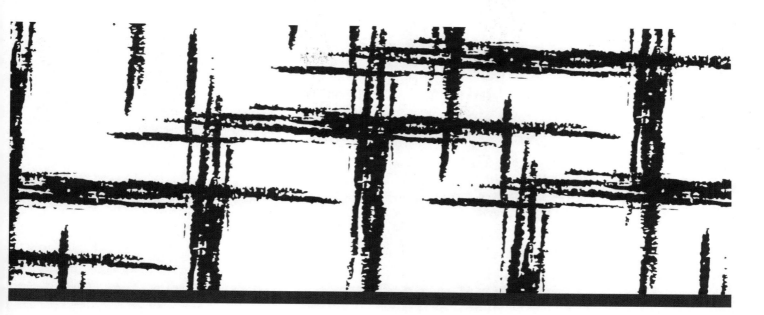

TOXIC NARCISSISTIC BEHAVIOR HURTS EVERYONE

THEY WANT YOUR ADMIRATION AND OBEDIENCE AS A PLAYER IN THEIR FAKE MAKE-BELIEVE WORLD.

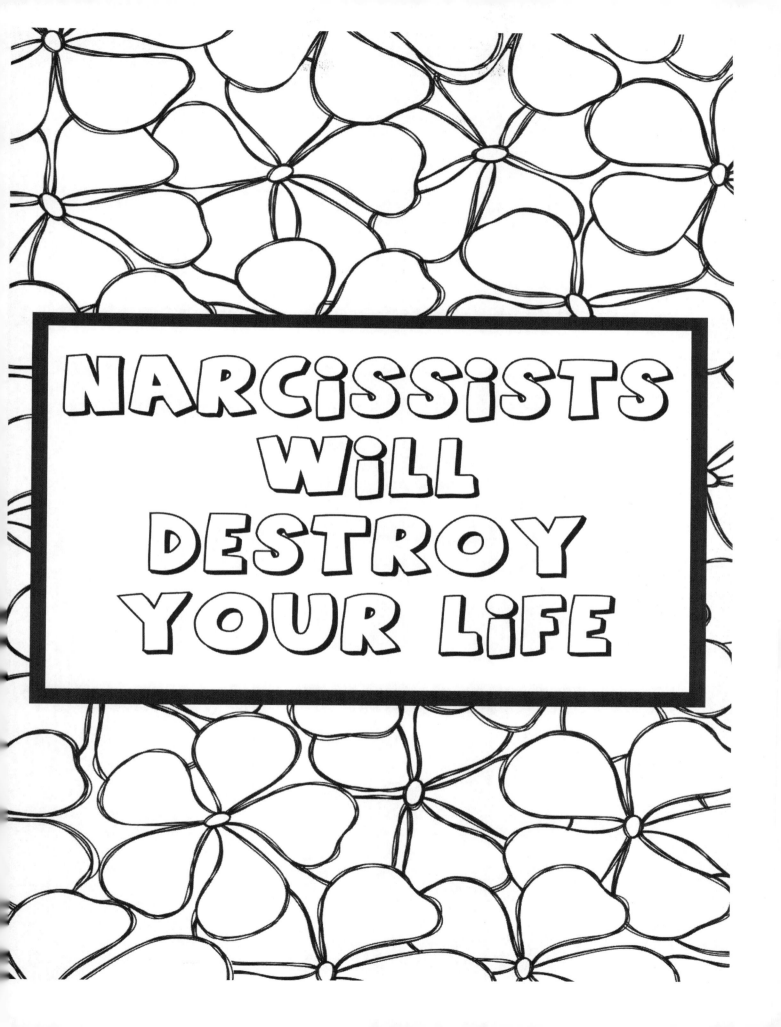

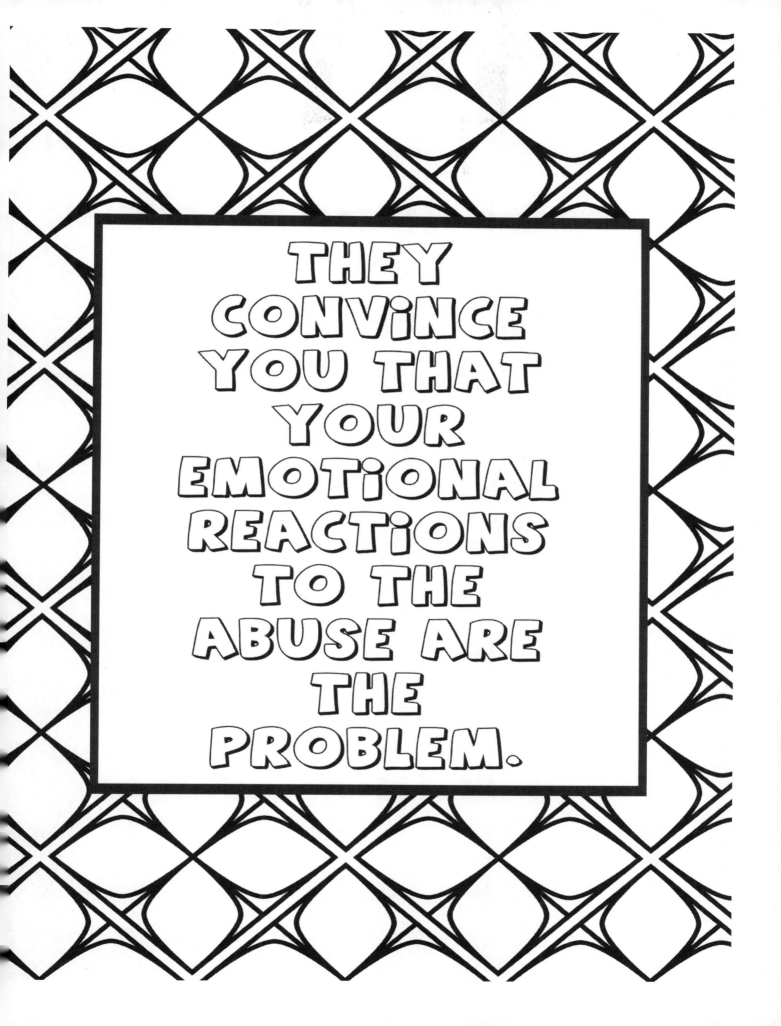

A NARCISSIST DOESN'T CARE HOW THEY MAKE YOU FEEL

YOU WILL NEVER REALLY SEE HOW TOXIC SOMEONE IS UNTIL YOU BREATHE FRESHER AIR.

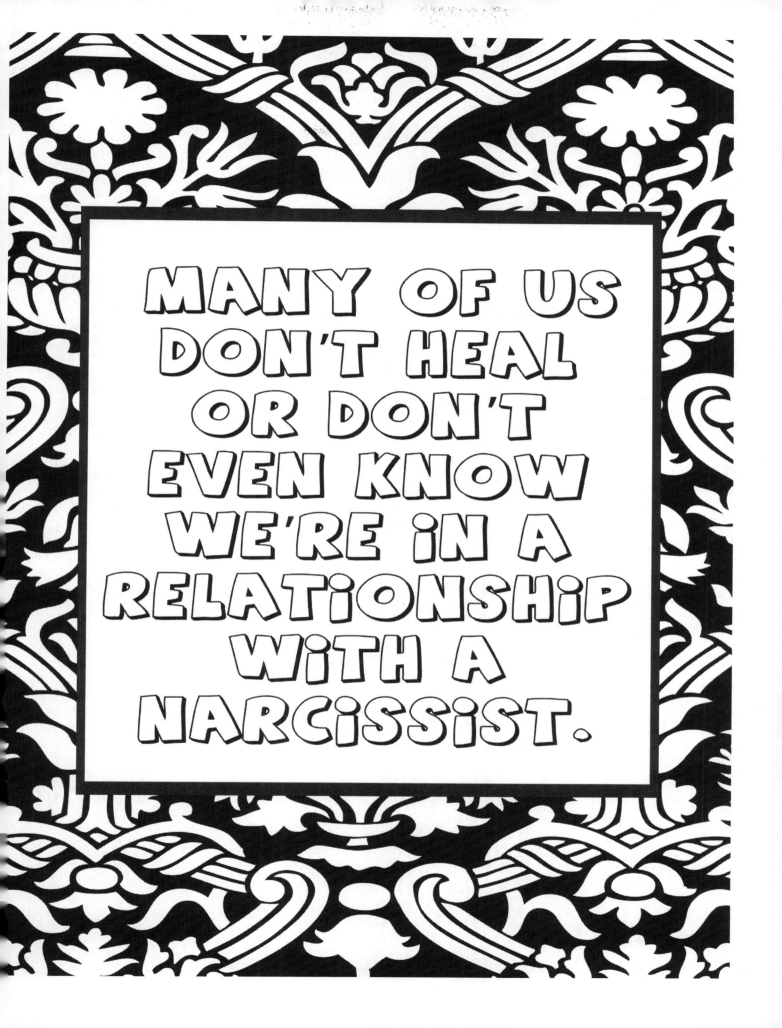

THEY WILL TELL YOU THAT YOU ARE OVERREACTING.

i FINALLY SEE RIGHT THROUGH THEM

RELATIONSHIPS WITH NARCISSISTS ONLY LAST FOR AS LONG AS YOU ARE WILLING TO PUT YOURSELF LAST.

DON'T LET NEGATIVE AND TOXIC PEOPLE RENT SPACE IN YOUR HEAD. RAISE THE RENT AND KICK THEM OUT.

THIS TOO SHALL PASS. IT MIGHT PASS LIKE A KIDNEY STONE, BUT IT WILL PASS.

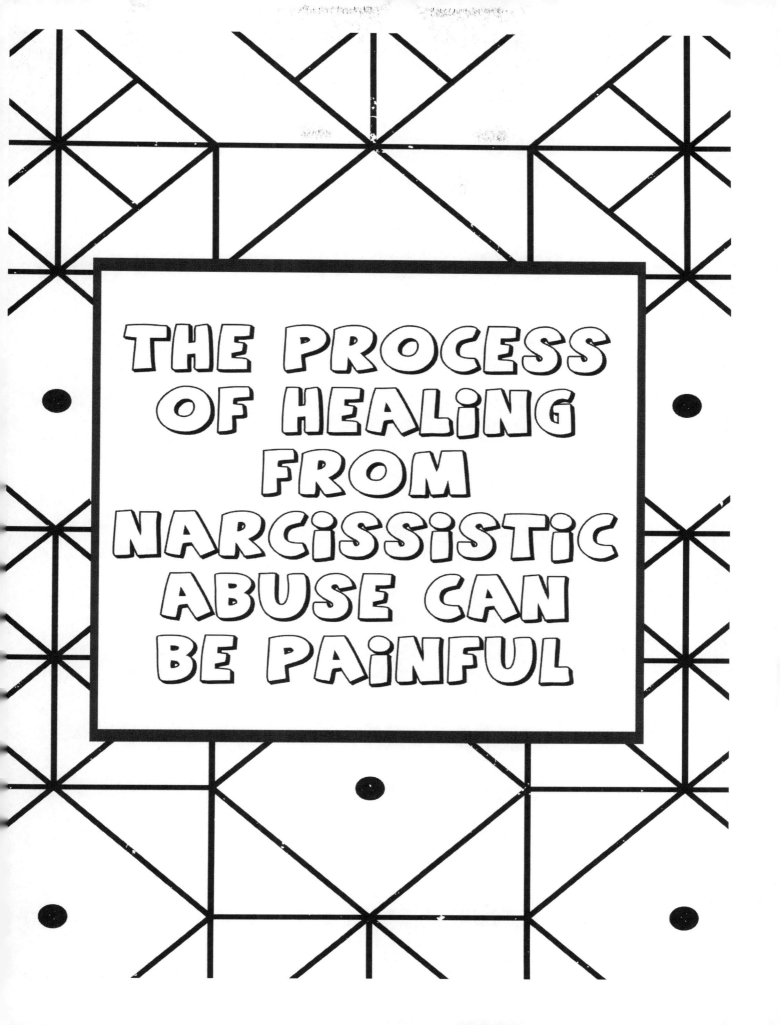

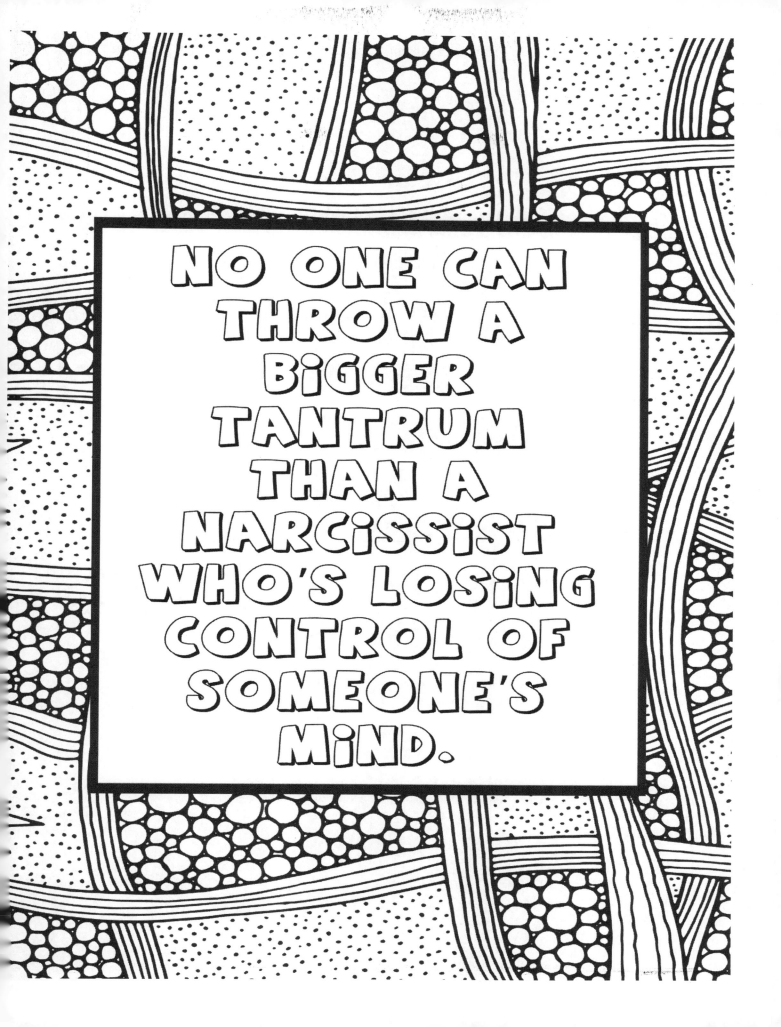

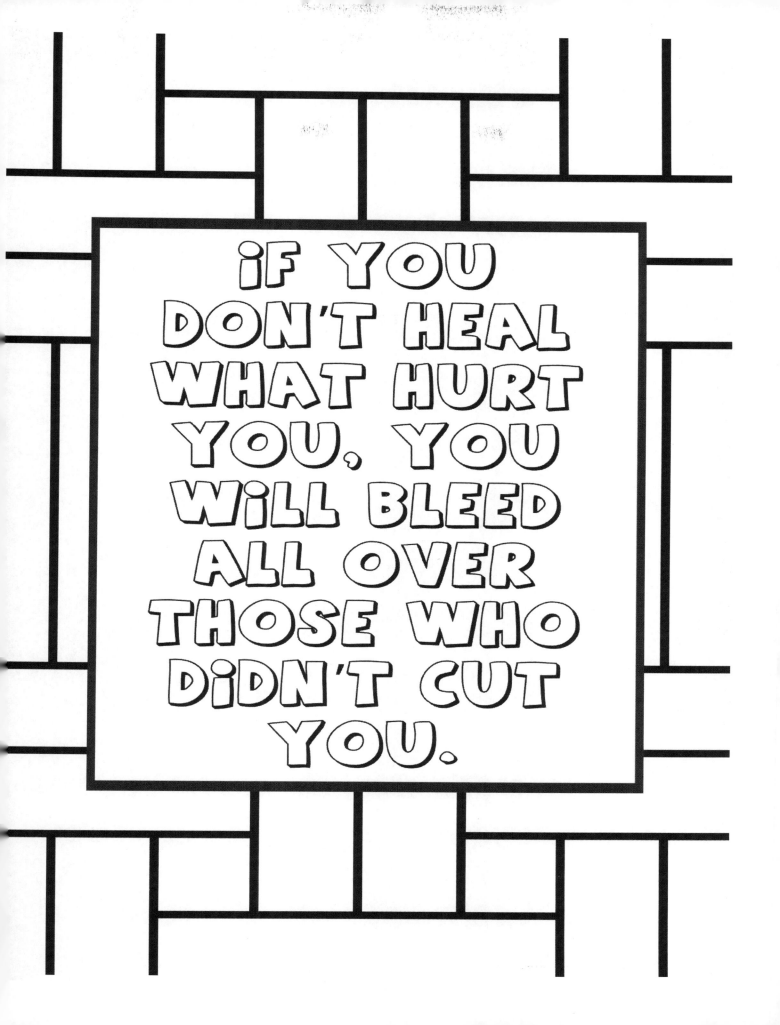

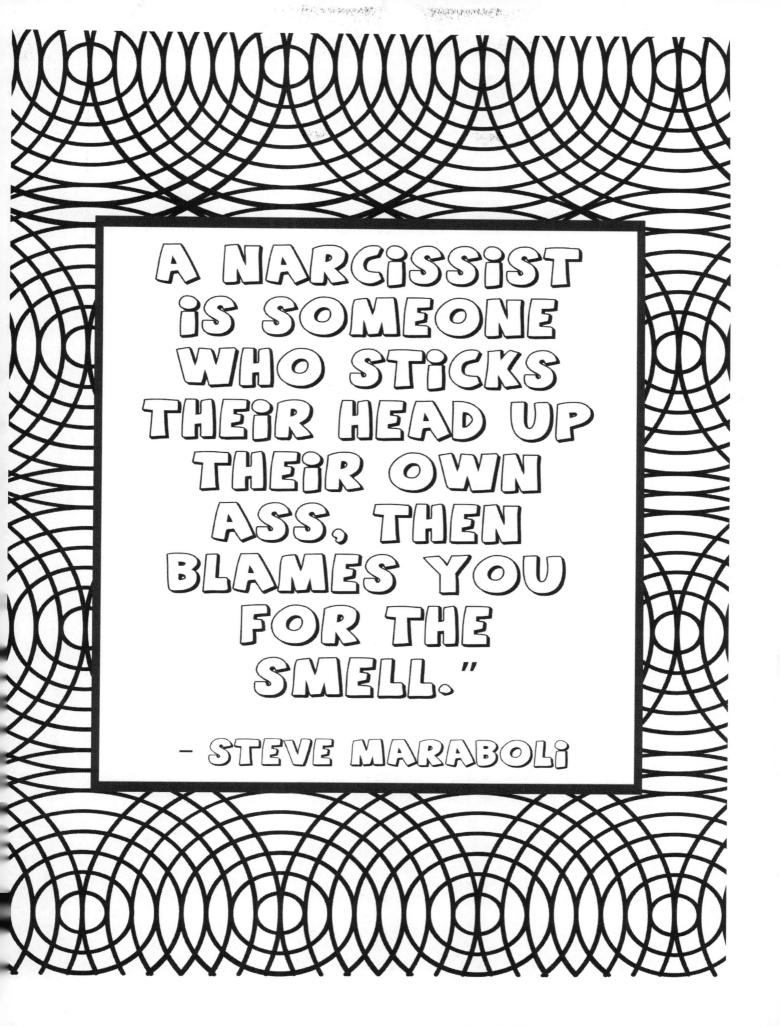

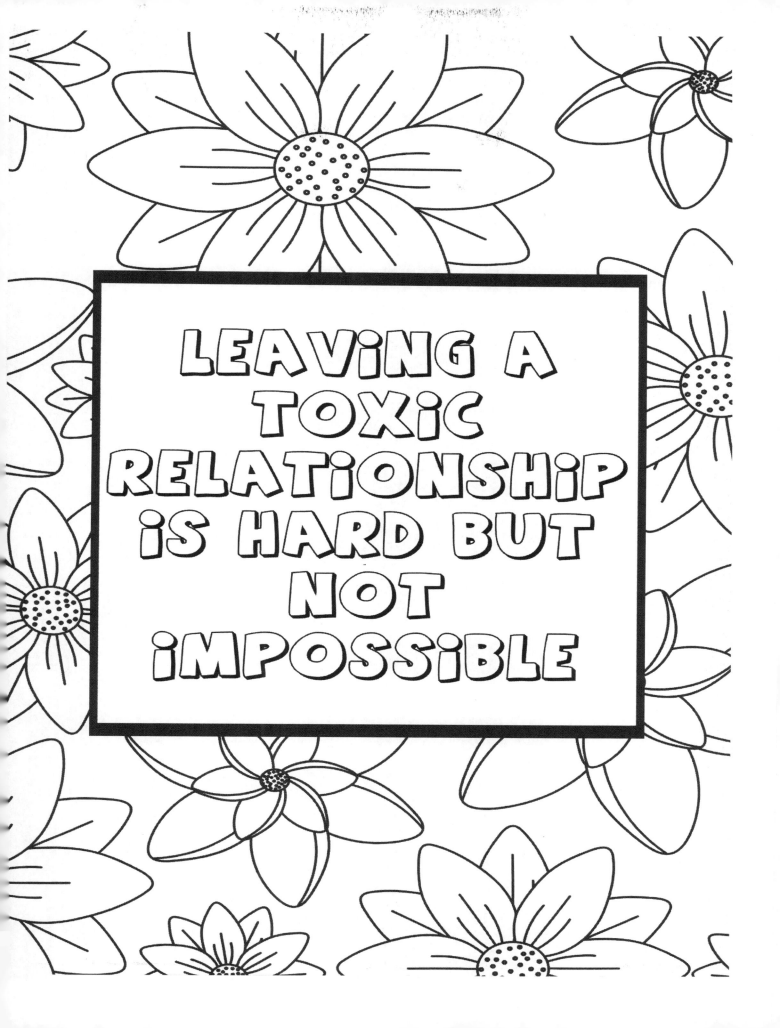

BEWARE. SOME PEOPLE WILL SELL YOU A DREAM AND DELIVER A NIGHTMARE.

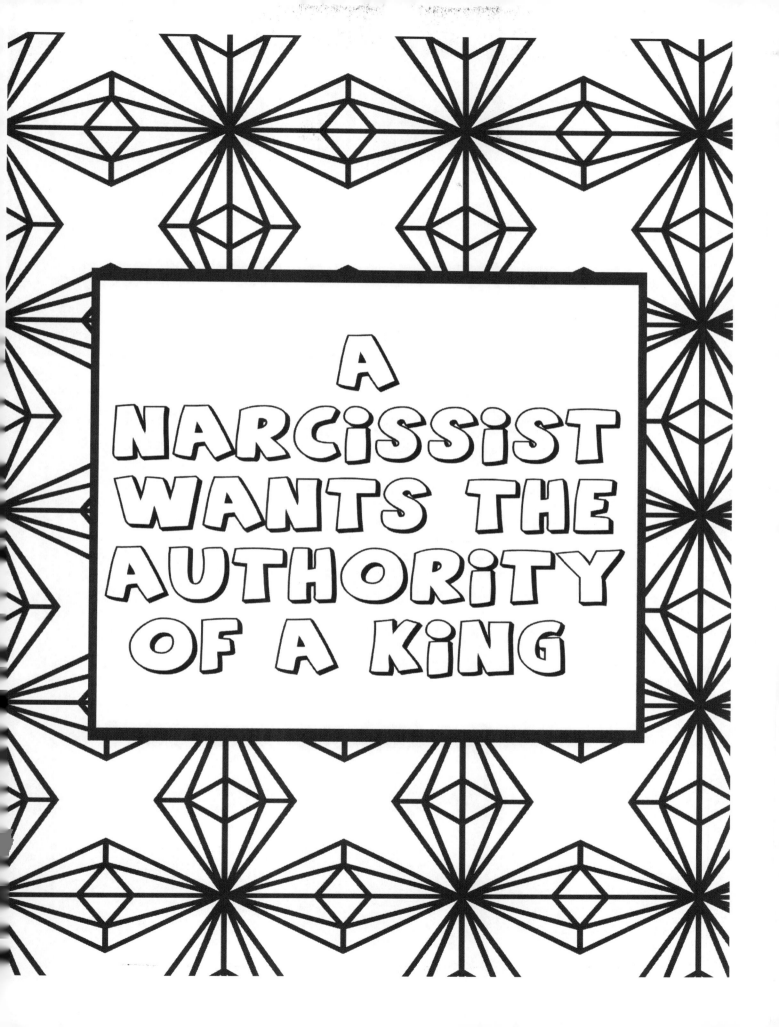

NARCISSISTIC PEOPLE DON'T WANT UNCONDITIONAL LOVE. THEY WANT UNCONDITIONAL TOLERANCE.

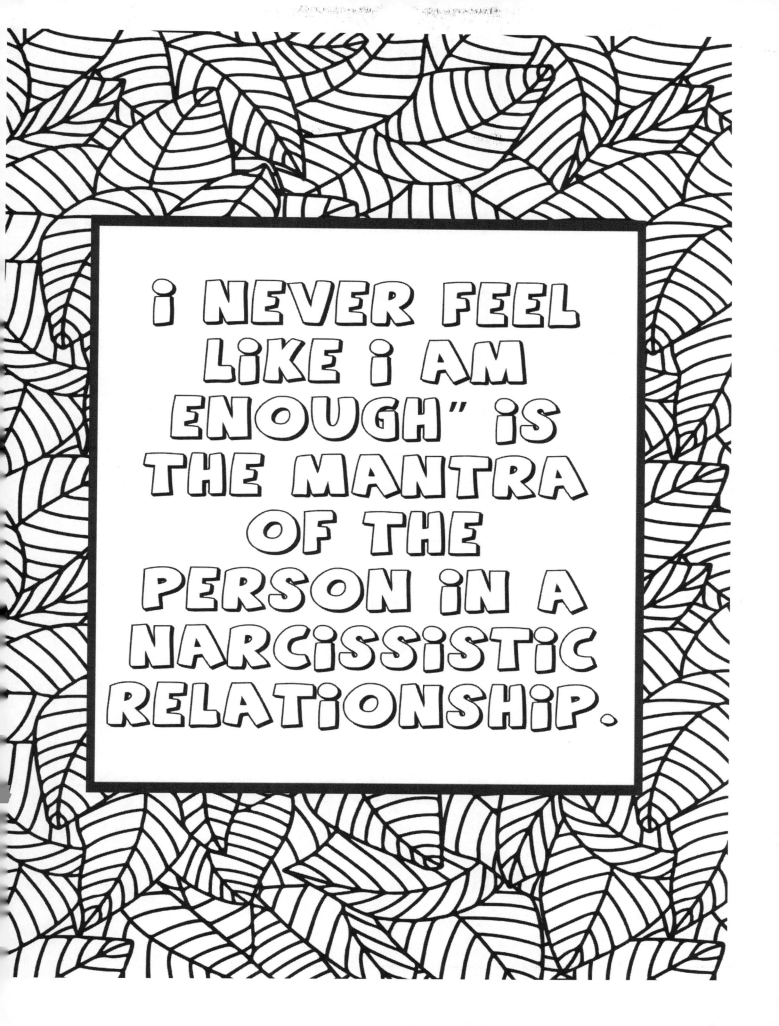

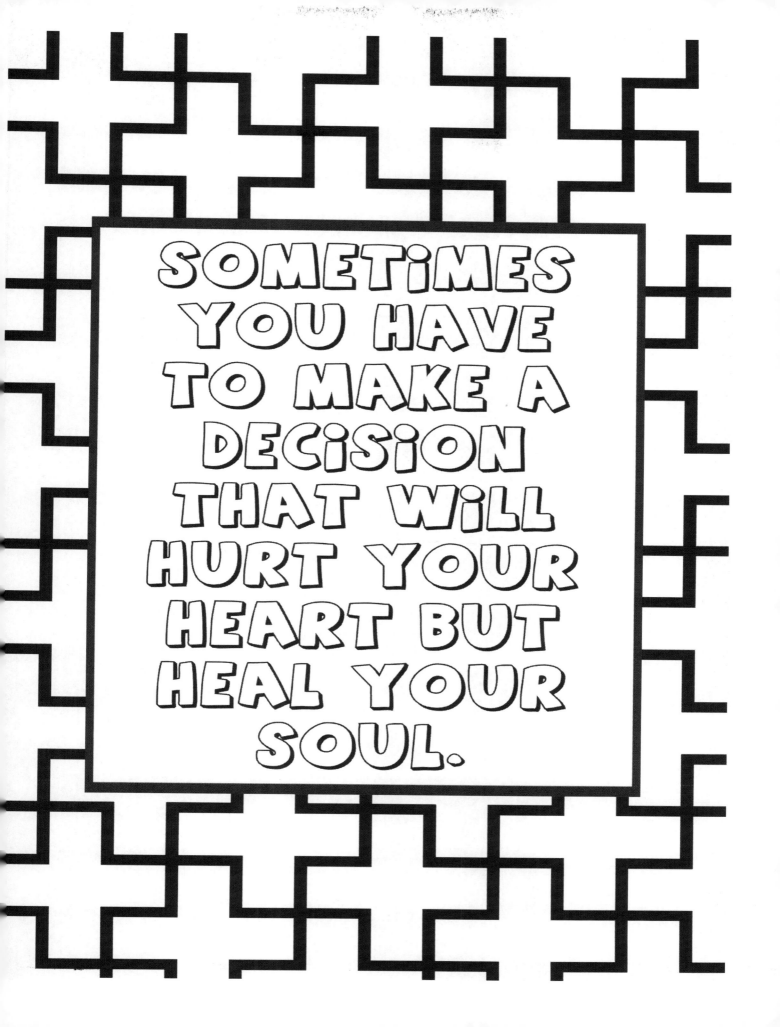

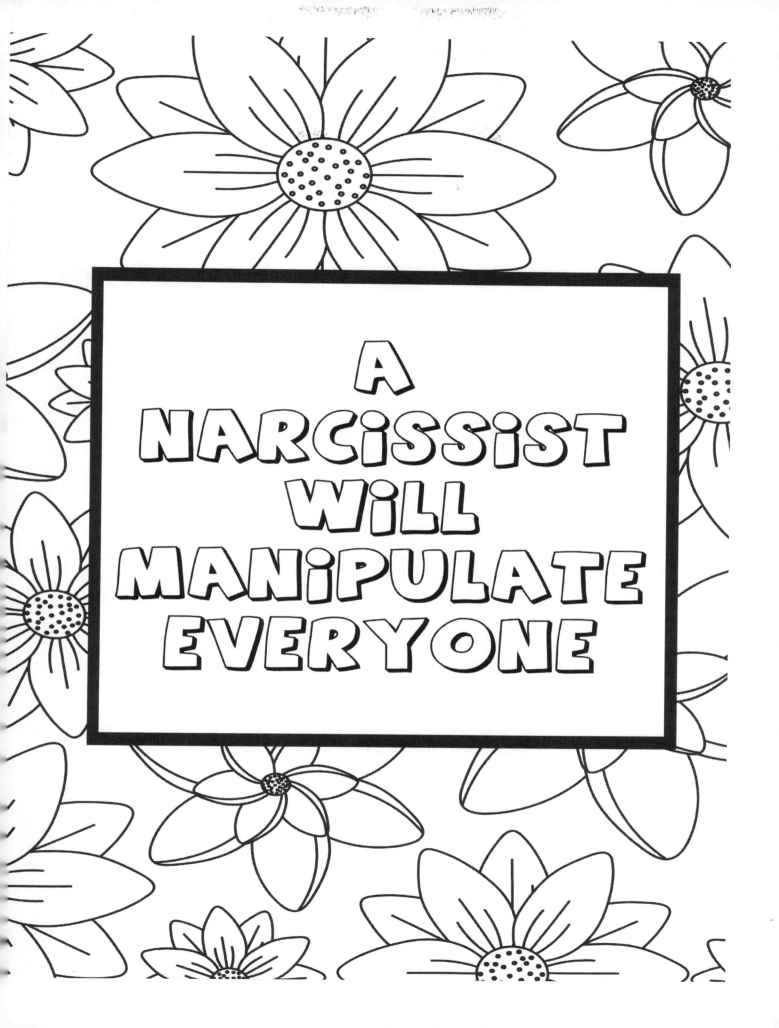

ALWAYS REMEMBER THERE IS HELP AND YOU ARE NEVER ALONE.

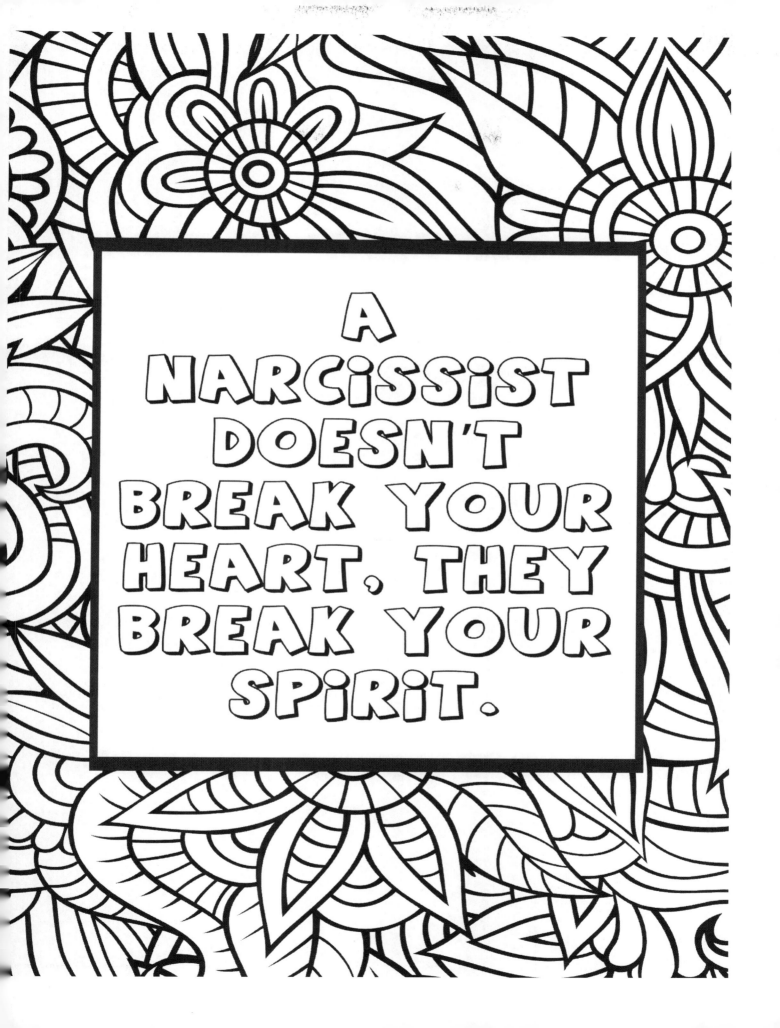

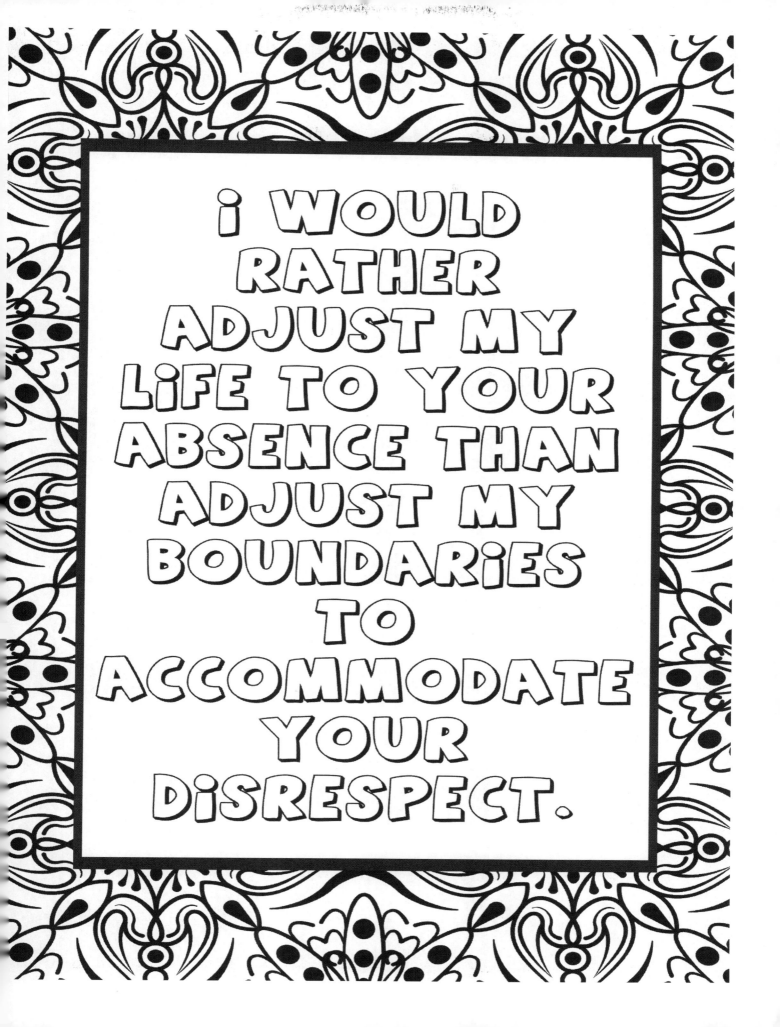

Printed in Great Britain
by Amazon